Young Albert Einstein

Young Albert Einstein

by Laurence Santrey
illustrated by Ellen Beier

Troll Associates

Library of Congress Cataloging-in-Publication Data

Santrey, Laurence.
   Young Albert Einstein / by Laurence Santrey; illustrated by Ellen
Beier.
       p.   cm.
   Summary: Examines the life of the physicist whose work
revolutionized scientific thinking, with an emphasis on his early
years.
   ISBN 0-8167-1777-X (lib. bdg.)   ISBN 0-8167-1778-8 (pbk.)
   1. Einstein, Albert, 1879-1955—Juvenile literature.
2. Physicists—Biography—Juvenile literature. [1. Einstein,
Albert, 1879-1955—Childhood and youth. 2. Physicists.] I. Beier,
Ellen, ill. II. Title.
QC16.E5S27 1990
530'.092—dc20
[B]
[92]   89-33940

Young
Albert Einstein

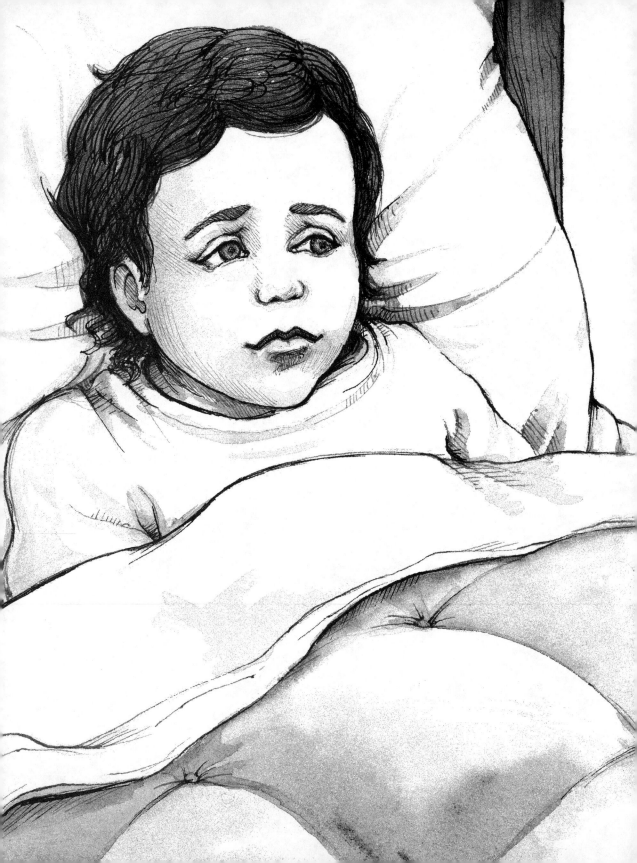

The five-year-old boy lay in bed, fighting the cold that had put him there for the last few days. He smiled as his father came into the bedroom. "Look at what I have for you, Albert," Hermann Einstein said, trying to cheer up his son. Mr. Einstein held out his hand. In it was something shiny and round—a magnetic compass.

Suddenly, the sniffles and fever didn't matter anymore to Albert. He was fascinated by the compass his father had given him, especially by the magnetic needle inside. It pointed straight north. And no matter in which direction Albert turned the compass, the needle still pointed in the same direction—north.

Albert played with the compass until his mother came in. She had seen the light underneath his door. "Albert, go to sleep." Her voice was soft and loving. "It is very late and you need to sleep to fight your cold."

The young boy obeyed his mother and slipped under the covers. But he kept the compass gripped tightly in his hand. It made him want to know so many things. Why did the needle always point north? Were there other toys like this one? Would they make you as happy as the compass? Make you think as hard? Why? How? What? So many questions filled Albert's mind as he drifted off to sleep.

Albert's parents, Paulina and Hermann
Einstein, also had questions. But they were about
Albert. Mr. and Mrs. Einstein were worried about
their son. Mr. Einstein asked his wife if she
thought something was wrong with Albert. After
all, the boy had not started to speak until he was
more than three years old. Even now, he did not
speak very much.

"We must not worry," Mrs. Einstein said. "The doctor examined him and told us there is nothing wrong. Just because he did not speak for so long does not mean he is dull-witted."

Her husband sighed. "Ah, well. We are not geniuses. So our son isn't one either."

Mr. Einstein was wrong. Albert *was* a genius, and in time the whole world would know it.

Albert Einstein was born on March 14, 1879, in Ulm, a small town in Germany. There, his father owned a small engineering business. Electricity had recently been discovered. All through Europe and America people were installing electric lights in houses and office buildings. Mr. Einstein's company supplied electrical equipment to customers in Ulm.

A smart businessman could have made a fortune in this new business. But Mr. Einstein didn't. He was always cheerful and full of hope. But he was not good at business. Within one year, the Einstein company failed.

The Einsteins were gloomy, but not for long. Mr. Einstein's brother, Jakob, wanted to help them. Jakob had an electrical supply business in the large city of Munich. He asked Albert's father to move there and become his partner. Jakob would take care of running the factory. Hermann, who got along so well with people, would deal with their customers. And so, Mr. and Mrs. Einstein and baby Albert moved into a small rented house in Munich.

Life in the city was good for the Einsteins. Many of their relatives lived nearby. There were weekly dinners and much visiting among the families. Munich was also a grand place to live. It had fine art galleries, concert halls, an opera house, and libraries. Hermann and Paulina Einstein enjoyed all of this. They loved music, literature, and art.

A year after the family moved to Munich, Mrs. Einstein gave birth to a second child, a girl. Two-year-old Albert bubbled happily about his new baby sister. He loved to watch the nursemaid tend to little Maja. He tickled his sister when she cried and was pleased to see her tears change to smiles. All through their lives, Albert and Maja were close friends. They understood and loved each other deeply.

The Einsteins were delighted that they had moved to Munich. The electrical business was very successful. And after a while, Hermann and Jakob bought a large piece of land in a suburb of the city. There, they built a double house. It was really two houses with no space separating them. And all around the joined houses was an enormous garden. It had large trees, play areas for the children, flower beds, and a small pond. The entire property was surrounded by a high wall.

The Einsteins enjoyed their lives. Most of all, they enjoyed being with each other—especially on Sundays. When he was in his sixties, Albert Einstein spoke fondly of a typical Sunday in his childhood. The day began with a spirited breakfast conversation about where to hike. Mrs. Einstein, as she usually did, picked the destination—a village or small town in the countryside near Munich. Then Mr. Einstein chose the route they would take.

Albert and Maja loved to listen to the plans
Mama and Papa made: which lake they would
stop at, what hills they would climb, and what
sights they would see. Mr. Einstein was in charge
of finding the "perfect" inn to eat at. It had to be
comfortable and serve good food. The excitement
built as the family planned for the adventure
ahead. And the Einstein children could never
remember a disappointing Sunday outing.

The walks the family enjoyed during Albert's youth gave him a love of the outdoors. As a young man, he continued to take long hikes. Sometimes he went with friends. Sometimes he walked out into the hills by himself. As he walked, he let his mind wander. He thought about nature, about time, about space, and about all the mysteries of the universe.

The scientific theories that would one day startle the world and make Albert famous were born during those long hikes. Even when the great Doctor Einstein was too old for difficult hikes, he still loved to get out and walk.

Another love Mr. and Mrs. Einstein gave their children was for music. Mrs. Einstein was a fine pianist. She played the piano every day, while Albert and Maja sat quietly and listened. She also believed that it was important for children to play musical instruments. So, at the age of six, Albert began taking violin lessons.

19

The youngster practiced at least an hour every day. The music delighted him, and he did his best to play it. But he was not a musical genius. Mrs. Einstein could hear that her son would never be a great musician. She could also see that he knew, deep down, that he had no special talent for the violin.

One day, Mrs. Einstein saw her son struggling to play a difficult piece of music. "Albert," she said, "only a few people in this world have that special spark that makes a brilliant musician. But music is also a thing of the heart. I do not play in a concert hall. I play my piano for my pleasure and for the pleasure of my family. For you the violin can be the same—an instrument that brings joy and inner peace."

Albert continued to take violin lessons and to practice. But his playing was just ordinary. Sometimes he even thought of giving up the instrument. However, he stayed with it. Then, when he was thirteen, something special happened.

Albert was practicing a piece of music by the great composer Wolfgang Amadeus Mozart. The teenager studied the musical score and suddenly began to see a pattern as pure as the mathematics he knew so well. It was a marvelous discovery for him. From that moment on, Albert Einstein played the violin with deeper understanding. He also found that playing music relaxed him and gave him pleasure. And for much of his life he played regularly.

Albert entered school when he was five years old. Most of the teachers at the school were kind, and the rules weren't too harsh. Albert was a quiet, patient, thoughtful boy. He often preferred to play by himself. During recess he was happy to build a many-leveled house out of wooden blocks. Or he would construct a house of cards

fourteen stories high. These things took time and a great amount of patience, but that suited Albert perfectly.

What Albert did not like were rough sports and military games. He did not like uniforms, toy guns and swords, the sound of a military band, or the sight of soldiers marching. Even as a child, Albert Einstein was a person of peace. He was to grow into an adult dedicated to the ideals of a peaceful world. In time, these ideals forced him to leave Germany forever.

Young Albert did well in elementary school. As Mrs. Einstein wrote to her mother in 1886, "Yesterday, Albert got his school marks. Again he is at the top of his class and got a brilliant record."

In 1889, when Albert was ten years old, he entered a secondary school called the Luitpold Gymnasium. The German gymnasium program is strongly academic. Students learn mathematics, science, modern languages, history, and ancient languages such as Latin and Greek.

Albert Einstein did not like the gymnasium.
The boys in the school had to memorize everything and were rarely allowed to ask questions.
Teachers spent the class time lecturing. Students
spent the class time writing down everything the
teachers said.

At Luitpold, a student who did not understand something was treated cruelly. When a teacher called on a student, the boy was expected to answer the question perfectly and in the teacher's exact words. A student who gave a wrong answer was made fun of by the teacher and laughed at by the other students.

The students were treated like little soldiers. They had to wear uniforms, stand or sit straight at all times, and march like troops from class to class. When they misbehaved, they were often punished physically.

Quiet, thoughtful Albert did not do well at the gymnasium. He disliked memorizing facts and rules. Years later he remembered: "As a pupil, I was neither particularly good nor bad. My principal weakness was a poor memory and especially a poor memory for words and texts."

Some of his teachers simply felt that Albert was a bad student. One of them, his Greek teacher, told him, "You will never amount to anything." On another occasion, Mr. Einstein asked the school's headmaster, "What profession should Albert consider?" The headmaster replied, "It doesn't matter, Mr. Einstein. He will never make a success of himself at anything."

What most of Albert's teachers did not know was that the boy was doing advanced work in mathematics by himself. It started when Jakob Einstein gave his young nephew a geometry book. Albert, who was twelve, was immediately drawn to the subject. It gave him endless hours of pleasure. Not since he had received the compass as a small child had the mind of Albert Einstein been so stimulated by anything.

Albert learned geometry by himself at a rapid rate. Because nobody told him what to think about the subject, he was free to think for himself. He questioned all of the facts in the geometry book. Where there were no answers, he had to figure them out for himself. Where there were answers, he had to figure out *if* they were true and *why* they were true.

At about the same time, Albert became interested in another important subject—philosophy.

It started when Max Talmey, a medical student,
became a regular dinner guest at the Einstein
home. This was in keeping with an old custom of
the Einstein family and other families of their
neighborhood. The custom was for each family to
feed a student once a week. That way, a student
without much money did not have to worry about
the cost of food that day. A student could eat at
a different family's house each day of the week.

Thursday was Talmey's day to eat with the
Einsteins. Albert looked forward to Thursdays
because Talmey talked to him about science and
philosophy. Philosophy is the study of the mean-
ing of life and the universe.

Talmey quickly recognized Albert's brilliance. The medical student gave Albert very challenging philosophy books to read. Albert read and then discussed them with Talmey. The thirteen-year-old began to think about things he had never thought about before. He wanted to know how the universe operated. He wanted to explore the laws of nature. He wanted to find answers to questions that had puzzled scientists and philosophers for centuries.

In a way, Albert Einstein was like Christopher Columbus. By traveling into the unknown, Columbus proved that the earth was not flat. And his daring discoveries opened the world to exploration and changed history in very important ways. Like Columbus, young Albert questioned the accepted ideas of his own age. Columbus knew there was more to be learned about the world's geography. Albert Einstein knew there was more to be learned about space and time.

But Einstein knew it was impossible to do physically what Columbus had done. It was impossible for him to travel to the stars and beyond. The only way to do that was in the mind. And so, Albert Einstein started studying the subject that was to become his life's work. By combining the questions of philosophy with mathematics, Einstein plunged into the science known as theoretical physics. It is a science that studies the physical world and tries to understand and describe the basic laws governing it through mathematics. Every form of matter, whether as small as atoms or as large as galaxies, is studied in theoretical physics.

Max Talmey was deeply impressed by young
Einstein. Years later, Talmey wrote, "Soon the
flight of Albert's mathematical genius was so high
that I could no longer follow."

In school, Albert did brilliantly in mathematics and philosophy. In his other subjects, however, he was below average. And he was not liked by his teachers. He often asked questions they could not answer. At times, he even challenged the strict discipline of the gymnasium.

As Albert was experiencing problems in school, his father was again experiencing problems in business. In 1894, the Einstein factory was closed, and Mr. Einstein was once more in need of financial help. This time, it came from a cousin of Mrs. Einstein. The family packed up and moved to Milan, Italy. There, Mrs. Einstein's cousin had opened a branch of the family business and asked Mr. Einstein to run it.

Albert remained behind in Munich. The fifteen-year-old boy moved into a room in a boarding house and continued his studies at the gymnasium. The family's plans were for him to finish the school year, get his diploma, and begin university studies. But these plans fell apart not long after the Einsteins moved to Milan.

Einstein described what happened. "I was summoned by my homeroom teacher who expressed the wish that I leave the school. To my remark that I had done nothing amiss, he replied only, 'Your mere presence spoils the respect of the class for me.'"

Albert was happy to leave the school and join his family in Italy. The next two years were among the happiest of his life. He visited museums, attended concerts, and read everything he could get his hands on.

Albert had already taught himself calculus and had developed a keen scientific curiosity. Even Jakob Einstein realized just how far advanced his nephew's learning was when young Albert solved an engineering problem that had delayed Jakob in constructing a machine. "You know," he later said to a close friend of Albert's, "it is really fabulous with my nephew. After I and my assistant engineer had been racking our brains for days, that young sprig had got the whole thing in scarcely fifteen minutes. You will hear of him yet."

During this same two-year period, Albert wrote his first scientific paper, which he sent to an uncle back in Germany. The subject of the paper was the relationship of electricity, magnetism, and ether. Most scientists of the time believed ether

was an invisible substance. It was said to fill space and carry electromagnetic waves. Young Albert was not ready to accept the existence of ether. He felt that the presence of ether had not been proven, and he said so in his paper.

In 1896, seventeen-year-old Albert entered the Swiss Federal Institute of Technology in Zurich. He majored in physics and planned to become a physics teacher. But he soon saw that the physics being taught at the institute was out of date. The teachers didn't know it yet, but Albert's private studies were far more advanced than their own.

Einstein graduated from the institute in 1900. Unfortunately, he had to give up the idea of teaching. His professors were annoyed by this student who told them that their thinking was behind the times. Not only wouldn't the institute hire him, but it also would not recommend him for a job at any other school.

In 1902, Einstein took a job at the Swiss Patent Office in Bern. He worked there for the next seven years, all the while studying physics and mathematics on his own. The result of this studying was a series of scientific papers. One of them, *A New Determination of the Sizes of Molecules*, Albert submitted as a doctoral thesis to the University of Zurich in 1905. At that time, scholarly papers of great merit could be accepted for a Doctor of Philosophy degree without a student having to go through years of formal classroom study. Einstein's paper was accepted by the university, and he received his degree. With it he could teach on the university level.

Another paper Albert wrote in 1905 contained his special theory of relativity. This theory is about uniform motion in a straight line, or speed that is constant. For example, suppose you are riding a train moving at a constant speed and drop a book. The book will drop straight down, not at an angle. You would get the same result if you stood still on level ground outside the train and dropped the book. So, as long as the train is moving at a constant, or uniform, speed, the mechanical activity of dropping the book will not be affected by the train's motion.

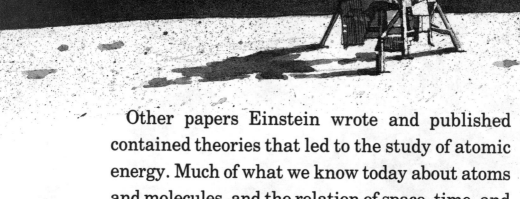

Other papers Einstein wrote and published contained theories that led to the study of atomic energy. Much of what we know today about atoms and molecules, and the relation of space, time, and the speed of light, comes from the ideas of Albert Einstein.

In 1921, Albert Einstein was awarded the Nobel Prize in Physics. By this time, he was already considered by many to be the greatest mind of the twentieth century. His ideas had revolutionized science. But they remained theory until World War Two. Only with the first experiments in nuclear fission were Einstein's theories made real.

One result of his work was the invention of the atom bomb, which helped to end World War Two. Other results have been the creation of radiation therapy to cure cancers, the development of the laser, and space exploration.

The last twenty-two years of Einstein's life, from 1933 until his death on April 18, 1955, were spent at the Institute for Advanced Study in Princeton, New Jersey. There in the quiet college town, Albert Einstein was a familiar sight to all. Every day, the kindly old gray-haired gentleman walked from his home to his office. Only when the weather was extremely hot or cold was he willing to travel in a car rather than walk.

The walks were Dr. Einstein's thinking times. But he was always ready to stop and speak with anyone who approached him. Even though he was widely considered the greatest genius of the twentieth century, he remained a truly modest man. Albert Einstein talked seriously with anyone of any age. He respected little children as much as the presidents, prime ministers, and Nobel Prize winners who visited him.

Albert Einstein also never abandoned his other childhood love, music. A number of his closest friends at Princeton's Institute for Advanced Study were amateur musicians like him. During the day the scientists worked on serious, scholarly problems. At night they played the music of Bach, Beethoven, Mozart, Brahms, and Mendelssohn. And when Dr. Einstein was finally too old to play the violin, he spent his evenings listening to the records of the music he loved. His mother's gift of music remained one of the constant delights of Albert Einstein's life.

As Columbus's discoveries opened up the New World, Einstein's work opened up the universe. Today scientists explore space, the origin of the universe, and the mysteries of the particles that make up the atom. These are studies made possible by the gentle, peace-loving genius, Albert Einstein.